LEADING WOMEN

Angela Merkel

First Woman
Chancellor of
Germany

TONYA MADDOX CUPP

Cavendish
Square

New York

*I dedicate this book to my amazing partner, Drew, my wonderful daughter, Laney, and my
incredible parents, Shirley and Dickie.*

Published in 2015 by Cavendish Square Publishing, LLC
243 5th Avenue, Suite 136, New York, NY 10016

Library of Congress Cataloging-in-Publication Data

Tonya Maddox Cupp.
Angela Merkel : first woman chancellor of Germany / Tonya Maddox Cupp.
pages cm. — (Leading women)
Includes bibliographical references and index.
ISBN 978-1-62712-978-7 (hardcover) ISBN 978-1-62712-980-0 (ebook)
1. Merkel, Angela, 1954- 2. Women prime ministers—Germany—Biography. 3. Christlich-
Demokratische Union Deutschlands—Biography. 4. Women—Political activity—Germany—
History—21st century. 5. Germany—Politics and government—21st century. I. Title.

DD290.33.M47C87 2014
943.088'3092—dc23
[B]

2014003453

Editorial Director: Dean Miller
Editor: Andrew Coddington
Senior Copy Editor: Wendy A. Reynolds
Art Director: Jeffrey Talbot
Designer: Amy Greenan/Joseph Macri
Photo Researcher: J8 Media
Production Manager: Jennifer Ryder-Talbot
Production Editor: David McNamara

The photographs in this book are used by permission and through the courtesy of: Cover
photo, 1, by Pascal Le Segretain/Getty Images; Antoine Antoniol/Getty Images, 4; US Army/File:-
Germany occupation zones with border.jpg/Wikimedia Commons, 7; A3500 Bernd Gurlt Deutsch
Presse Agentur/Newscom, 10; Popperfoto/Getty Images, 13; JOHANNES EISELE/AFP/GETTY
IMAGES/Newscom, 18; Marvel/File:Leipziger City-Hochhaus.jpg/Wikimedia Commons, 22; JdH/
File:Curie-nobel-portrait-2-600.jpg/Wikimedia Commons, 28; Unknown photographer, Reproduc-
tion by Lear 21/File:Thefalloftheberlinwall1989.JPG/Wikimedia Commons, 31; AFP/Getty Images,
34; Ulrich Baumgarten/Getty Images, 36; Andreas Rentz/Getty Images, 40; Thomas Imo/Photothek/
Getty Images, 44; Sean Gallup/Getty Images, 46; Guido Bergmann/dpa/picture-alliance/Newscom,
49; Roland Magunia /DDP/Getty Images, 51; Pool/Getty Images, 52; Adam Berry/Getty Images, 57;
Sean Gallup/Getty Images, 59; DigitalGlobe/Getty Images, 63; Sean Gallup/Getty Images, 64; Sean
Gallup/Getty Images, 67; AFP/Getty Images, 69; Johannes Eisele /AFP/Getty Images, 70; File:Euro-
pean union map 2005-06-02.png/Wikimedia Commons, 73; Carsten Koall/Getty Images, 87.

Printed in the United States of America

CONTENTS

Mercredi 19 février 2014

CHAPTER ONE

Growing Up in East Germany

"Step by step."

I t's one of Angela Merkel's favorite sayings, and it describes her approach as Germany's **chancellor**. Some people call her deliberate; others call her indecisive. She isn't known just as *Chancellor Dr. Angela Merkel*, either: Angie, Mutti, the Merkel Mystery, the Merkelator, the Decider, Queen of Europe, and Iron Lady have all been monikers for this remarkable woman. Regardless of how she's perceived, in November 2005, Angela Merkel made history by becoming Germany's first woman chancellor. Before that, however, history made Angela Merkel. The country she grew up in, the country she has lead, has had a complicated, volatile past. That volatility started well before she was born, but its effects continue into the present.

Post-World War II Germany

Just nine years before Merkel was born, her country was involved in a war that would prove among the deadliest and most destructive in all history: World War II. After losing the war in 1945 to the Allies, Germany was split into four zones, with each being governed by a foreign nation: the United States, Great Britain, and France (who together composed the western Allies), and their eastern Ally, the Soviet Union (USSR), which consisted of modern-day Russia and other neighboring countries. Berlin, the country's capital, was also quartered, although it was deep in the Soviet Union's bloc.

The Allies initially planned on treating the zones as a single country, but differences in the Soviet Union's approach began taking their toll. The U.S., France, and Great Britain based their governance on democratic **capitalism**, an ideology that advocated freedom through individual choice. The USSR, however, governed according to **communism**, a system in which all individuals were expected to contribute their goods and labor to the common good. The USSR's version of communism manifested itself in dictatorship. Volumes have been written about the histories between—and the approaches taken by—these nations, but these two different approaches proved incompatible.

The rift between the democratic capitalists and communists might have become too wide when the

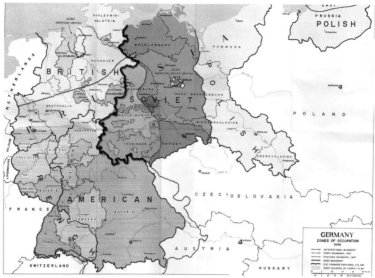

A post-WWII Germany map shows the four Allied zones: Great Britain, France, U.S., and USSR. Berlin is shown within the Soviet territory.

western Allies implemented new currency, called the ***Deutschmark***, without notifying the USSR. The Deutschmark was named after the Germans' word for their country, ***Deutschland***. In an effort to evict the western Allies, Soviet Union leader Joseph Stalin blocked all traffic, including railway, road, and canal access, and stopped supplies to Berlin. Two days later, in June 1948, the western Allies began the Berlin Airlift. The United States Air Force, the British Royal Air Force, the Royal Canadian Air Force, the Royal Australian Air Force, the Royal New Zealand Air Force, and the South African Air Force dropped supplies, including food and coal for fuel, to the isolated Berlin citizens. In May 1949, the Soviet Union agreed to allow supplies, but the airlift continued until September 1949.

That same month, the western Allies established the **Federal Republic of Germany (FRG)**. In response, the Soviet Union established its **German Democratic Republic (GDR)** in October 1949. Germany was divided in two: the democratic West and communist East. Angela Merkel was more than a year old before West Germany was declared a sovereign nation and the Allied occupation ended.

The Kasner Family and Protestantism in the GDR

Born Angela Dorothea Kasner, Germany's future chancellor came into the world on July 17, 1954. Soon after her birth, her father, Horst Kasner, moved the family across the border into East Germany, where they lived until West and East Germany were reunited in 1990. Horst Kasner's Protestant pastorship called for him to relocate to East Germany when most people were moving to democratic West Germany. Her father explained the unlikely move to totalitarian, communist East Germany by saying, "We were young and idealistic back then," and that pastors were needed in the East. Merkel's brother Marcus was born three years later, and her sister Irene, ten years later—which made them East German nationals by birth.

The family mostly lived in Templin, about an hour north of Berlin, where he taught theological students at a cluster of buildings called *Waldhof*. Merkel's childhood

Communism Deconstructed

Communism often has negative connotations. Historically, communist nations have also been dictatorships. However, the concept itself is based on equality and doesn't necessarily imply totalitarianism. The communist ideal is for everyone in a community to own and have responsibility for the means of production, including factories and natural resources, in order to prevent exploitation by a few privileged individuals. Private property is the exception, not the rule, in a communist culture. Instead of one small group of people owning most of the businesses and earning most of the money, all resources are divided up equally among citizens. There is some debate about how communism and **socialism** differ—and whether they even do.

Many people dispute whether communism is a viable economic system, and those who argue that it is not point to the collapsed communist Soviet Union as an example. Critics argue that communism has a history of rewarding mediocrity, bucking the human desire to own, or not meeting anyone's needs in an effort to meet everyone's needs.

Anti-communist feelings are so strong that, even as late as 2013, Angela Merkel had been "accused" of promoting the ideology. In response, Merkel says, "What is important to me is that I never tried to hide anything."

home was their school, as well as a school for younger students with disabilities. Merkel explains that, aside from whatever happened politically in the GDR,

"I have been shaped by parents and I am proud of that as well."

A young Angela Merkel cooks over an open fire while camping with friends in the summer of 1973, before she entered the University of Leipzig. She often traveled with friends.

The East and West German split politicized everything, including religion. The GDR allowed Protestants to practice their religion as long as they complied completely with the communist government.

In fact, although the founder of communist ideology, Karl Marx, famously called religion the "opiate of the masses" and incompatible with communism, the East German government actually worked with the Protestant clergy to implement their communist policies among the people. Although this seems contradictory, some churches, including Horst Kasner's, put together a document titled *Seven Propositions on the Freedom of the Church to Serve* that outlined how communism and religion should coexist for church members and others in the community. One of those propositions was the idea that cooperating with the German Democratic Republic was something Christians must do as their duty.

Merkel explains that her father "had a very logical, very rational approach to things." According to journalist Andrew Marr, Merkel's father agreed with socialism but disagreed with the dictatorship. While the East German government allowed him to perform his duties as a Protestant pastor, Horst Kasner knew they were also always watching both him and his family to ensure they did not use his position to speak out against their regime. For example, his wife, Herlind Kasner, wasn't allowed to teach English and Latin. Government officials were afraid that she, as a former West German citizen, might negatively influence any East German students she taught.

In fact, despite his outward support of communism, there was indeed speculation within the East German government that Horst Kasner actually held other views.

Kasner frequently held meetings at his school for what some called "left-wing intellectuals." Once, in 1968, Kasner's group discussed anti-Soviet dissident and human rights activist Andrei Sakharov, a Russian nuclear physicist who called for capitalism and communism to coexist peacefully. When the *Stasi*, East Germany's secret police force, heard about this, they called Kasner in for questioning. The Stasi told Kasner that participating in such discussions was a criminal act, but that they would not press charges if he agreed to become one of their informants—individuals who provided insider information about neighbors, colleagues, friends, or even family members suspected of doing or saying

The Stasi

The German Democratic Republic's Ministry for State Security, commonly known as the Stasi, was the East German secret police. Members of the Stasi relentlessly spied on GDR citizens to keep them submissive to the government. They bored holes in apartment walls, planted recorders in bathrooms, and demanded to know who hosted overnight guests. Those suspected of illegal actively could be imprisoned and tortured. Additionally, the Stasi used informants, some of whom were Protestant clergy members and community officials. Some accounts claim that there was one informer for every seven citizens.

something that could be seen as a criminal act against the government. Despite the pressure, Horst Kasner refused to cooperate with them.

The Berlin Wall

In 1961, when Merkel was seven years old, the East Berlin government began building a wall between itself and West Berlin, dividing a city—and indeed, the world—between communist and capitalist. Families living on opposite sides of the Berlin Wall would be kept from each other for years, and in some cases never saw each other again. Merkel describes the day the Wall went up: "Everybody was stunned... That was my first memory of political events." That Sunday, Horst Kasner pastored a service. After the service, "everybody was crying," says Merkel.

A family watches as East German border guards add barbed wire to the Berlin Wall. East Germany's government began building the Wall in July 1961. It came to symbolize the Cold War.

13

The Death Strip

Physically, the Berlin Wall started as barbed wire. The GDR government wanted to keep East Berliners from defecting to the West, but the barbed wire wasn't enough to stop them. The Wall split many families, and people continued to try to escape. The GDR government wanted to put a stop to it.

They started by replacing the barbed wire with concrete. Over the years, additional complicated and dangerous barriers were added in various places along the barrier. A signal fence alerted the guards if someone touched it. The GDR added steel spikes, which they referred to as "surface obstacles," at the bottom of the fence to impale anyone who might successfully climb over it. If they got past the road where soldiers patrolled, they had to make it into and back out of a deep ditch—a "tank trap"—whose purpose was to snare vehicles that might try to barrel through the barrier. Railroad tracks were welded together and wrapped with barbed wire, and another ditch was ready to trap escapees. Dogs were put in runs. Buildings near the Wall were torn down to facilitate "a clear field of fire." A concrete wall over eleven feet tall, painted white to help spot an escapee, was the final obstacle in a person's attempt to escape to West Berlin. Lights shone on the border throughout the night. Soldiers with guns occupied observation towers that were stationed about every 820 feet (250 meters). This section of the Wall became known as the Death Strip.

On August 13, 1962, demonstrators protested the one-year anniversary of the Berlin Wall. But for some, protesting was not enough. Two eighteen-year-old construction workers working on a site nearby had noticed a carpenter's workshop that stood very close to the Wall's Death Strip. On August 17, during their lunch break, they hid in the building, and then jumped from a window over the first line of barbed wire. The young men then ran through the Death Strip toward the Wall while soldiers shot at them. One of them, Helmut Kulbeik, made it across. The other, Peter Fechter, was shot. He was just ten yards from it when a bullet from a machine gun hit him in the pelvis. Fechter lay on the ground for fifty minutes while soldiers and citizens alike watched, neither side coming to help. When Fechter died, East Berlin soldiers carried away his body.

Over 100 East German people died at the Wall while trying to escape. Some were killed and some committed suicide. Angela Merkel knows that it sounds like ancient history and so unlikely as to be impossible, but she also knows better: "When I talk to younger people, I realize how far away they are on the Wall and the lack of freedom of that time. [For them, the Wall] is about what it was like when my parents talked about the Second World War."

GDR leader Walter Ulbricht ordered the Berlin Wall be built to prevent any more people from fleeing East Germany for West Germany. It began with physical barriers, such as barbed wire, and eventually became a 100-mile (161-kilometers) concrete barrier fortified by armed guards. GDR and Stasi officials refused to admit that the guards were ordered to kill potential **defectors** on site, but an official order has been found that confirms these orders: "Don't hesitate to use your weapon even when border breaches happen with women and children, which traitors have often exploited in the past."

Besides eluding the Stasi's oppression, reasons for leaving the GDR were numerous. For one, supply shortages were common in the GDR. They were so common that reporter Dorothy Miller said in 1962 that food shortages were "no longer news" but that the government had "violently denied" requiring rations. Miller explained: "[I]f regular ration cards were issued, the authorities would have to commit themselves to a certain amount of meat per head per week. They are apparently not in a position to guarantee this minimum, and therefore limit themselves to 'customers' lists,' a so-called 'cold' form of rationing." Limiting how much food each family could purchase would reveal a problem that the GDR government would not admit existed. They were fearful of being perceived as weak by the rest of the world.

In a 2010 interview with German newspaper *Bild am Sonntag*, Merkel explained that when she was growing up in East Germany, "you had to be very alert and organized. Going into a shop you looked first to see what goods people were buying at the checkout, then searched for them yourself." Even twenty years later, Merkel said that she has bought items she doesn't even need, simply because she can.

"This penchant for stockpiling lies somewhere deeply inside me, because living amid the shortages [in the GDR] you just took whatever you could get."

In a 2013 newspaper interview, Merkel was asked if she remembers ever wanting to leave the GDR. She replied, "I quite frequently thought about leaving. Some of my acquaintances had fled from the GDR... I talked to my parents... [but t]he sense of belonging with family and friends always prevailed at the end. I did not want to let them down, and I did not want to be alone. It was very important for me to know that if there were an emergency, we could have left the GDR and started over in West Germany. But we didn't delude ourselves, because emigration applications were complicated." Still, despite the difficulties of living in the GDR, Merkel is grateful for her childhood, saying,

"My parents raised us with much love and gave us access to a broad education."

Horst and Herlind Kasner raised Angela and her brother and sister in Templin, East Germany. Here they are watching in 2005 while their daughter is voted chancellor.

Attending School

As a child, Angela Merkel faced the usual personal struggles of growing up, separate from the economic and political issues of her day. While she was strong academically, for example, Merkel lacked athletic skills. Once when she was nine, it took her forty-five minutes to muster the courage to jump off a diving board. Perhaps her lack of physical agility is one reason science, math, and languages appealed more to her. She excelled in them. Merkel attended the *Erweiterte Oberschule*, a selective secondary school, and in an interview, one of Merkel's teachers described her as "really gifted in languages." She began studying Russian in fifth grade, and was part of a language club. She even won the Russian language Olympics.

A practical and cautious person by all accounts, young Angela preferred a quiet and orderly approach to life. School friend Hartmut Hohensee remembers, "She was very quiet—a rather plain and mousy girl. But very nice, and friendly, and extraordinarily intelligent." She spent school holidays in Berlin with her grandmother, with whom she enjoyed visiting museums. In her spare time, she collected modern art postcards. Young Angela also had a propensity to plan Christmas shopping two months before the holiday, though not necessarily out of excitement: "I always wanted to know what I'd face," she says. "Structuring my life and avoiding chaos was more important."

One of the benefits of her father's profession was that it allowed the Kasner family to travel outside of East Germany on occasion. At age fourteen, she traveled to Czechoslovakia with her family, and during the tenth grade she made a repeat visit, and visited Romania and Bulgaria as well.

When Merkel was young, she also joined the GDR's **Freie Deutsche Jugend (FDJ)**. This young people's organization is described as promoting socialism, but Merkel says she joined for community reasons, and helped schedule and sell tickets to book readings. Merkel's parents had encouraged her to join the organization hoping that it would provide her with more opportunities.

When Merkel became chancellor, a former coworker accused her of working for the Agitation and Propaganda portion of the FDJ, which was "responsible for brainwashing in the sense of Marxism…" Many people still fear and suspect communism, and despite Merkel's insistence that her participation in the FDJ was far from ideological, some people have criticized Merkel's FJD membership as late as 2013.

Merkel seemed well on her way to success. However, during her last year in grammar school she did something completely out of character, as well as unthinkable in East Germany in the 1970s: She rebelled. As a thinly veiled political statement, she and a group of students collected money for the Mozambique Liberation Front, otherwise known as Fremilo, who were trying to oust

Mozambique's foreign occupiers—occupiers that were similar to the USSR occupiers in East Germany at the time. The students also sang in English, the language of Western democracy. This offense was almost enough to get her banned from attending university after her graduation from the Erweiterte Oberschule, but Horst Kasner used his work connections to help ensure this did not happen. Still, she had come dangerously close to wrecking her future. To avoid further trouble, she decided to occupy herself with the study of physics.

CHAPTER TWO

Young Adult Life

Despite the fact that students at the time were not expected or pushed to excel at school, Merkel graduated from the Erweiterte Oberschule in 1973 and was granted permission to attend a university. She wanted to get away, and she did just that. She left Berlin to attend the University of Leipzig, a city about 170 miles (274 km) south of Templin. The coming years would bring even more mobility to her life, and although West and East Germany remained split and very different, things were about to change drastically.

Attending the University of Leipzig

Between government restrictions and Merkel's affiliation with the church, her educational and career choices were limited in totalitarian East Germany. Merkel chose to focus on her love of science. She liked that science was based on facts, something the German Democratic Republic couldn't twist to advance its agenda. She also enjoyed the challenge the field provided: Physics was the only subject she had ever failed. Her strength lay in understanding theories. Perhaps that was a way for her to reconcile faith with science. She said once that mankind has "developed such a technical skill that he must also develop in parallel its capacity for abstraction, must look beyond his own nose and his own life." She also said,

> *"If we do not learn humanity, mankind will have to pay for it in a dramatic way."*

Merkel lacked discipline during the beginning of her university studies. With no one there to remind her, she would often forget to eat dinner, or eat incredibly late after having woken, hungry, in the middle of the night. She realized that she had the freedom to do as she wished, but missed having the usual barriers that provided structure.

To earn money, she took part-time jobs in and around the campus. For example, she was a bartender at a dance club located in the university's physics building. Authorities told the club's management that the music they played must be at least 40 percent German.

They defied the rule, and the students who came danced mostly to Western music, including disco, which was popular then. She also did laundry, and once had to iron shirts for the Russian army. After a few splurges on childhood whims like cherry and apple juice, which had been hard to come by when she was little, she gradually became very selective about how she spent her earnings. She found that once she had some spending money and the autonomy to buy what she wanted, she no longer wanted it so badly.

Merkel also spent her money on travel. At that time, travel to other European countries from the GDR was rare and highly controlled by the government. When Merkel was at university, she used her status as a physics student to study abroad whenever she could. Merkel often visited the Soviet Union, as well as the Heyrovský Institute in Czechoslovakia's capital of Prague, to conduct research, sometimes spending months away.

She met her first husband on such a trip. In 1974, Angela Kasner entered an exchange program and met Ulrich Merkel, another physics student. Ulrich said he liked Angela "because she was a very friendly, open, and natural girl" who was incredibly intelligent, energetic, and ambitious. They moved in together two years later, but after a while realized that having a marriage license would make it even easier to both find work and live together in bureaucratic East Germany. Although he was an atheist, Ulrich agreed to a church wedding in Angela's hometown of Templin in 1977. There are those who wonder if Angela married Ulrich because of how much easier it made living in the German Democratic Republic. Angela herself has said that getting married for practical reasons instead of romantic love was common then.

The newlyweds' Berlin living quarters were tight. They had a 100-square-foot studio apartment, and they shared a bathroom with other occupants. They often visited her parents, as well as his. The marriage didn't last long, however. The couple separated in 1981 to Ulrich's surprise when Angela moved out, and divorced in 1982. Although Angela has never spoken frankly in public about their relationship, Ulrich has said that it was better that they parted ways because things had changed between them.

East Berlin had a housing shortage at the time her relationship with Ulrich ended, so she and some of her friends broke into an abandoned apartment building and moved in. Because she didn't have a permit to live in the building, Merkel was considered a squatter—a person living in a building illegally. She kept traveling despite her dubious living conditions, and hitchhiked with friends through the Soviet Union, staying in cheap hotels. Thanks to her fluency in Russian, she was able to avoid many of the common travel restrictions placed on East German travelers at the time.

When she completed her physics degree at the University of Leipzig in 1978, she began looking for work in her field. She applied for a job, and her application drew the notice of the Stasi, who called her in for questioning. They said she could have the job if she agreed to be an informant for them. Merkel's calculated response was one she learned from her parents. She told them she "couldn't keep secrets." The irony was that she could, of course—all East German residents learned to do that very thing. They knew the secret police were everywhere, and they chose confidantes carefully.

Practicing Physics in Berlin

After receiving her undergraduate degree, Merkel moved from Leipzig to East Berlin. From 1978 to 1989, she did graduate work at the Central Institute for Physical Chemistry of the Academy of Sciences. The prestigious institute, known in Germany as *Zentralinstitut fur physikalische Chemie*, employed over 600 people. Merkel was the only woman in the quantum chemistry department. She had no complaints about it, saying:

"The only thing that I used to dislike about being a scientist was not having much opportunity to speak to others during the day."

At the time, even academic careers were subject to the whims of the GDR government. A person with

Marie Curie: Merkel's Role Model

Merkel once said, "Even if you study something quite different, it's worthwhile to spend some time delving into the late 19th and early 20th century period. This was when Marie Curie discovered radioactivity." Physicist Marie Curie, who was born in Poland in 1867, is Angela Merkel's role model. The two scientists have a lot in common. Like Merkel, Curie's mother was a teacher, and Curie herself lived in an oppressive country. Polish citizens were spied on, as the Stasi spied on the citizens of the GDR, and they "knew that a single conversation in Polish, or an imprudent word, might seriously harm not only themselves but also their families."

In her twenties, Curie left Poland and studied at the Sorbonne, a well-respected university in Paris, France. There, she received her degree and met Pierre Curie, whom she would later marry. They did much research together and struggled with poor conditions and equipment (as did Merkel in the GDR). Despite what they lacked, the Curies were able to isolate two radioactive elements, radium and polonium, which they named after Marie's native Poland. She further studied the radiation emitted by the elements and found that, in addition to causing cancer, they could help cure it as well.

Marie and Pierre Curie shared the Nobel Prize for Physics in 1903 with Henri Becquerel. Becquerel discovered spontaneous radiation, and the Curies continued researching it. That year, Marie Curie became the first woman ever to win the Nobel Prize. When her husband passed away in 1906, she became the first woman to head the physics lab at the Sorbonne. Curie was also the director at the University of Paris's Radium Institute, where she later took a professorship. Curie won the Nobel Prize for Chemistry in 1911 for her work with radioactivity. In 1934, she died of a blood disease caused by radiation.

skills and intelligence as strong as those attending the Academy couldn't always be sure they would be allowed to complete their studies and receive their doctorate degrees. Some groups were charged with inventing or discovering something that would give communist governments an advantage over capitalist governments. Merkel and her fellow scientists studying quantum chemistry were given more latitude than other scientists when it came to their research. Their department wasn't paramount to communism's potential success.

As a theoretical physicist, Merkel investigated the decay of hydrocarbon molecules. She completed her doctoral thesis and earned a PhD in physics from the Academy of Sciences in 1986. The title of her doctorate thesis translates as, *Study of the mechanism of decomposition reactions with simple bond breaking and calculation of their rate constants on the basis of quantum-chemical and statistical methods.* In the thesis' foreword, Merkel thanked a man named Joachim Sauer for his "critical insight." Merkel and Sauer met when she was a student and he was teaching at the Academy, and the two would later marry.

Around this time, Merkel received special permission to attend a cousin's wedding in the city of Hamburg, which was located in the democratic half of Germany. She had not been to West Germany since the building of the Berlin Wall nearly three decades earlier.

East and West Germans celebrate the fall of the Berlin Wall. It had stood for twenty-eight years before the USSR's *perestroika* helped make Germany's reunification possible.

The Wall Comes Down

While Merkel was earning her degree, communism and the government of the German Democratic Republic had been weakening. In March 1985, Mikhail Gorbachev became the leader of the Soviet Union. Gorbachev encouraged *glasnost*, an increased openness and transparency in government institutions and activities in the USSR that was completely lacking before he came to power. He also championed *perestroika*, a restructuring of the Soviet Union's political and economic system.

In 1988, Gorbachev reversed the Brezhnev Doctrine, which had allowed the Soviet Union to defend communist power in any eastern European country. With President Ronald Reagan, Gorbachev helped end the Cold War between the United States and the Soviet Union. (The Cold War was so called because there was political tension, but no actual fighting.)

While Gorbachev was working to reform Soviet communism, protests against the dictatorship in East Germany became more common. The GDR government tried to concede to some wishes without letting go of its entire structure by permitting its citizens to travel. That policy snowballed with a mistake made on November 9, 1989, when a radio reporter incorrectly announced that citizens could travel without any restrictions. The checkpoints were quickly flooded with people. The following day, people brought hammers, sledgehammers, and chisels, and began to physically pick apart the Berlin Wall. It was a massive celebration and the beginning of a new era.

When she heard the news, thirty-five-year-old Angela Merkel was elated. First, she called her mother, Herlind. She explained that cross-border travel was going to be allowed, and reminded Herlind of a long-standing agreement they'd made when Angela was younger: to eat oysters together at a hotel in West Berlin. However, as practical and cautious as ever, Merkel stayed well away from the initial fray at the border crossing, and urged her family to do the same. Instead of grabbing a hammer and heading to the Wall to help tear it down, she went out for a drink, wound up celebrating with strangers at an apartment building, and went home. She realized that change—even positive change—takes time. History proved her right: despite the destruction of the Berlin Wall, it would be a year before West and East Germany were officially reunited. Still, as the Berlin Wall came down, a deep desire to help shape what her country would become arose in Merkel.

> *"The new freedom and the many new possibilities awakened in me the curiosity and desire to actively participate in the changes."*

A Marriage That Lasts

When the Berlin Wall came down in 1989, Angela Merkel and Joachim Sauer were in a relationship. When they first met at the Academy of Sciences in 1981, she had been a graduate physics student, and he was teaching at the Academy. Merkel's divorce from her first husband became final in 1982. Sauer separated from his first wife in 1983, and they consequently divorced in 1985. Merkel and Sauer then lived together for several years before they married privately in 1998. What attracted her to Sauer? According to Merkel, her husband is authentic and enjoys occasional silence, traits that she appreciates.

Joachim Sauer and Angela Merkel (in 1989 and 2007, respectively) knew each other at the Academy of Sciences. Years later, the two scientists lived together and married.

A world-class scientist, Joachim Sauer prefers a life outside of the political spotlight, though he does sometimes travel with Merkel on government business trips, often to the United Kingdom. While he was with her when she received the Presidential Medal of Freedom in 2011, he chose not to attend her 2005 inauguration, which caused some people to raise their eyebrows. The dry-witted Merkel explained that if his absence were likely to cause a diplomatic incident, Sauer would have attended. He has been known not to fly on a government plane to avoid incurring a fee, and this frugal approach seems consistent with the **Eurozone crisis**-based policies Merkel is famous for. His frugality isn't just about money, though: Once when he was offered an official German vehicle for travel, Sauer took the subway instead.

Merkel and Sauer have no children. However, Sauer does have two sons with his first wife, and Merkel and Sauer are grandparents. They enjoy traveling on vacation together, and both are opera fans. And, although Sauer chooses to live a private life, he does play an important role for the first woman chancellor of Germany—that of a confidant and sounding board. Merkel explains that, when she is in need of advice, "My husband is a good corrective."

CHAPTER THREE

From Scientist to Politician

W hat compelled Dr. Angela Merkel to leave science and pursue politics? The Berlin Wall had fallen. Everything was changing. She thought the new Germany needed someone who had never been in politics before. Some critics have implied that Merkel had a grand political plan. She claims that this is not the case, however. She has said that, for her, just the act of "Making a speech was a big step."

Few could have imagined the trajectory of this quiet scientist-turned-politician. Photographer Herlinde Koelbl first met Angela Merkel in 1991 when she was creating *Spuren der Macht* (*Traces of Power*) a years-long portrait collection of politicians as they rose in power. According to Koelbl, Merkel "was shy, maybe a little bit awkward. She was never vain. And that's unusual in politics." Over the years, Koelbl noted that Merkel changed and became more confident. By all accounts, Merkel's was an abbreviated ride to great power.

Choosing Sides

In 1989, thirty-five-year-old Merkel joined the Democratic Awakening (DA) party, in part because she liked its name. From there, her political career seemed to gather steam from being in the right place at the right time with the right skills. For example, the West German government had provided the party with new computers, and Merkel was one of the few who knew how to help set them up. While unpacking computers wasn't exactly what she'd had in mind when she entered politics, it was a start, and she made the most of it. In early 1990, she was again tapped to troubleshoot when a DA party representative who was scheduled to meet with journalists had to miss the appointment, and she was asked to fill in at the last minute. As if overnight, Merkel wound up becoming the Democratic Awakening press officer, a position that required her to be in the public eye.

The life of the Democratic Awakening as an autonomous political party was brief, however. The DA party merged first into the Alliance for Germany, and eventually with East Germany's existing **Christian Democratic Union (CDU)** party, whose counterpart had a lot of influence in West German politics.

East and West Germany weren't officially politically reunified yet, and the GDR held its first (and only) free election in March 1990, separate from those held in West Germany. When CDU politician Lothar de Maizière won the democratic election for chairperson, he wanted to hire someone from the DA as the party's deputy spokesperson. Angela Merkel had worked as DA press secretary for just four months, but de Maizière hired her as CDU deputy spokesperson anyway. (It didn't hurt that de Maizière's father knew Horst Kasner, Merkel's father.) Reunification was coming fast and furious at this point, and de Maizière has said that Merkel always tried to work well with all involved parties.

Merkel preferred working behind the scenes to the glare of the political spotlight. This was possibly in large part an aftereffect of growing up in a dictatorship, during which she'd had to remain quiet for her safety. However, she wasn't allowed to remain quiet when she entered politics. Matthias Gehler, who worked with Merkel when she was the Alliance for Germany spokesperson, said, "I was her boss, and up to this point Merkel had acted very much in the background. And you had to tell her, from time to time, 'Angela, you'll have to speak at the podium, too.' And then she did."

German Government

Germany has a **parliamentary** system of government. The legislative body is split between two houses: the *Bundestag*, or the lower house, and the *Bundesrat*, or the upper house. (*Bundes*, pronounced BOON-dess, translates to "nation;" *tag* to "day;" *rat* to "advice.") The Bundesrat members are chosen from and are appointed by the sixteen *Länder*, or states. A Länder's population determines how many representatives it sends to the Bundesrat. Like the United States, Germany struggles to balance the needs of the individual states with the country as a whole.

Bundestag members are elected directly and indirectly by eligible citizens at least eighteen years old. Citizens vote by district and make two choices—one for a specific person and one for a political party. Almost 300 Bundestag members are directly voted for, and the other half makes its way there based on how many votes its political party received in the election. If a party gets less than 5 percent of the total party vote, it doesn't get to participate in the Bundestag. This method, called *proportional representation*, is designed to ensure that the government heeds smaller, less powerful groups while not being directed by more extreme fringe groups.

Just as the party makeup of the German parliament changes, its size fluctuates, too. A party receives *overhang votes* if additional members are directly voted in during an election. Overhang votes are essentially extra seats to account for the additional votes. After an election, it takes one or two months for the parties to form agreements, or **coalitions**, between each other to be formally agreed upon. Afterward, the German parliament meets to elect the nation's chancellor.

A *chancellor* is chosen every four years. German citizens don't directly vote for their chancellor. Instead, their Bundestag members vote for a chancellor from among their existing members. Voting for chancellor requires 300 votes unless there are overhang seats. In that case, one more than half the total seats are required to seal the vote for chancellor.

"Kohl's Girl"

After East and West Germany officially reunified in 1990, then German chancellor Helmut Kohl was in search of a quiet East German woman—preferably a Protestant—who could serve as a member of his cabinet. He looked first to the CDU party, of which he was a longstanding and active member, and was told that Angela Merkel might fit the bill. After meeting with her, an impressed Kohl guaranteed Merkel that he would make her a committee chair upon her election to the Bundestag, the lower house of Germany's Parliament or legislative body. She won in the December 1990 election. Merkel had been a member of the Christian Democratic Union for less than a year, and yet she was about to take a position in the national government.

Kohl referred to Angela Merkel as *das Mädchen*— "The Girl"—and would come to be her political mentor. He first appointed Merkel to a position he considered fairly unimportant: the Federal Minister for Women and Youth. She worked within that ministry from 1991 to 1994, focusing on issues such as funding for kindergarten education. In 1994, she became Federal Minister for Environmental Protection and Security of Reactors, a post she retained until 1998. During both assignments, she also simultaneously served as the acting CDU chairperson.

Merkel lost her ministerial appointments in 1998 when Kohl lost the chancellorship in a federal election to Gerhard Schröder. The same year, however, she was appointed as CDU general secretary and, later, its chairperson. Merkel continued on with the Christian Democratic Union because she believed the party best balanced the interests of all its constituents—younger and older people, women and men, employees and employers. Of her party's work, Merkel said,

"It is not always easy to get everyone under one roof, but rewarding... This is important to me."

Kohl's Mistake

Shortly after being ousted as chancellor in 1998, the news broke that Kohl, who was still a member of parliament and the CDU, had illegally accepted donations. Some Parliament members wanted to keep the situation private, but "Kohl's girl" insisted on calling out her mentor publicly, on the front page of the newspaper. She submitted a letter, published in *Frankfurter Allgemeine Zeitung*, calling for Kohl's resignation. Translated, part of the letter reads:

> [A]n accurate historical picture can emerge only on a foundation of truthfulness. We can only build a future on a foundation of truthfulness. Helmut Kohl must accept this

realization; the CDU must accept this realization. Incidentally, only by doing so will the party manage to avoid exposing itself to attack every time another news item about alleged donations surfaces.

Merkel knew it would require a major effort to separate Kohl from the CDU after his twenty-five year chairmanship. In her letter, she said that she recognized that it might be "asking too much" of Kohl to expect him to immediately leave office and relinquish all his responsibilities.

Although Merkel's tone sought to protect the integrity of her party, many Germans and those in the media saw unexpressed motives and character attached to her public letter: She wanted more power. She was disposing of someone who could no longer help her advance. She was calculating.

Former German chancellor Helmut Kohl with future chancellor Angela Merkel in 1992.

In the wake of the Kohl scandal, the Christian Democratic Union's reputation suffered temporarily, but not by much. Months later, in April 2000, Merkel was elected CDU chairperson. Then, the 2002 chancellorship went to a candidate from the CDU's sister group, the Christian Social Union (CSU): Edmund Stoiber. Merkel was poised to run for chancellor at the time, but instead settled for CDU secretary-general and eventual leader.

Becoming Chancellor

From 1998 to 2005, the chancellorship belonged to Social Democratic Party (SPD) member Gerhard Schröder. Schröder's tenure was rocky, however. He made changes that were so unpopular that his party experienced huge losses during local elections. With his own influence and the influence of his party quickly slipping, he unexpectedly requested that Germany have its federal elections in 2005, a year earlier than planned. When the CDU nominated Angela Merkel for the chancellorship, Schröder said publicly that he was sure Merkel would not win—but, fearing a last-minute rebellion within his own party, ultimately urged his fellow Social Democrats to vote for her.

Angela Merkel was elected chancellor, and her election marked a number of firsts. Not only was she the first East German to hold the position in reunified Germany, Merkel was also the first woman to ever hold the position. She would be reelected in 2009, and again in 2013.

Angela Merkel is sworn in for a third term as Germany's chancellor. She made history in 2005 as the first woman and the first East German to be elected chancellor.

What confluence of events and characteristics propelled this woman into such a powerful position, despite her lack of early political ambition or training? What now most influences her decisions as chancellor? It all comes down to one thing, Merkel has said:

> *"As far as I have been shaped by politics, I have been shaped by German reunification... I am proud to be a politician for all of Germany with East German roots."*

Fighting Sexism While in Office

When Merkel worked for chancellor Helmut Kohl, there were few women leaders within the Christian Democratic Union party, and she was often faced with sexism. German Cabinet Minister Ursula von der Leyen said that often at the beginning of Merkel's career, men tried to humiliate her by being authoritarian and loud. von der Leyen said she "realized that [Merkel] let them have their way, but she was very soft. Answering in a low voice. This was a behavior where men at the very beginning couldn't cope with—at all—because that was not the typical thing to do." Even as chancellor, she is not immune from such sexism. Merkel, her office manager Beate Baumann, and head of media relations Eva Christiansen work closely together. The three are often disparagingly called "the girls' camp" by the German media.

Later in her career, a woman from another party once asked Merkel whether she noticed that female politicians were scrutinized more than men about their appearance. Merkel said that that scrutiny had become part of her life. In fact, Lothar de Maizière, who worked with Merkel when she was the CDU spokesperson, was quoted as saying Merkel's appearance was "awkward" because she was wearing sandals, loose skirts, and short hair, but that Merkel "didn't seem to care." He even asked one of his female office managers if she would go clothes shopping with Merkel.

Merkel mostly dismisses or ignores the comments on her appearance, but her sense of humor was on full display in June 2011. Merkel presented to U.S. Secretary of State Hillary Clinton a framed *Frankfurter Allgemeine* newspaper front page. The photo cropped out their heads, focused on their hands and suits, and asked if readers could tell the difference between Clinton and Merkel. Two women world leaders met and it made the front page—via their appearance. It is interesting to note that when she shared this joke with Clinton, Merkel was in Washington, D.C., to receive the Presidential Medal of Freedom, which is the highest U.S. award a civilian can earn.

Her body and hair have also been criticized—or ignored, as they were when, in early 2009, Mattel created an Angela Merkel Barbie doll for its fiftieth anniversary. Mattel, it would seem, wanted to honor Germany's first female chancellor as a role model for girls. However, most people had trouble recognizing her, as the doll simply looked like Barbie with cropped hair and a pantsuit. In response to its Merkel makeover, Mattel simply declared that Barbie "inspired girls to believe they can be anything."

Merkel's approach (or non-approach) to women's issues has earned criticism as well, and not only from opposing parties. For years she was against efforts in the **European Union** to impose a legal minimum of women as company board directors. Then, when

Former U.S. Secretary of State Hillary Clinton and Chancellor Angela
Merkel draw comparisons based on their gender and wardrobes.
Their politics are not similar, but both have a sense of humor.

companies lagged behind on their promise to employ
more women, Merkel revised her opinion and voted for
the *Frauenquote*, or "female ratio." By 2016, companies
in the German stock exchange are required to have at
least 30 percent women on their board of directors;
large companies are required to create plans that shift
more women into executive roles. She said companies
were responsible for hiring more women for middle-
management positions as well, so they would be prepared

for higher positions later. As a physicist, Dr. Merkel also urged young women and girls to get involved in science and engineering because of how well paid those positions are. Merkel made it clear that the quota wasn't the end-all be-all in addressing workplace inequalities:

"Overall, we have to advertise it again and again: The most successful companies are the companies where men and women, where people of different ages, work well together."

The Angela Merkel Barbie was Mattel's attempt to simultaneously honor Merkel's influence on girls and celebrate the doll's fiftieth anniversary. The Merkel version wasn't mass-produced.

CHAPTER FOUR

Chancellorship

Different political parties have played varying important roles in Angela Merkel's political life. As a member of the Christian Democratic Union, she has been able to pretty much count on backing from the Christian Social Union as well. They, along with the Social Democratic Party (SPD), helped her get elected as chancellor in 2005. When she ran for the office, former chancellor Gerhard Schröder encouraged SPD party members to vote for Merkel in 2005 so they could create a coalition. It worked.

When Merkel first took office, she knew she had a lot to learn. Since her training was in physics, not politics, Merkel asked British Prime Minister Tony Blair if he would show her the ropes. Merkel also made sure she surrounded herself with people who specialized in the ins and outs of politics. Thomas de Maizière (the cousin of Merkel's former boss, Lothar de Maizière), whom she would later make her interior minister, had apprenticed with Blair and passed on his expertise. With de Maizière's help, Merkel learned everything from scheduling, advisor searches, and secret service management, to broader legislative processes.

The Eurozone Crisis

Things weren't ideal when Angela Merkel became chancellor. Merkel originally planned to reduce business regulation, reform welfare, and cut taxes to help the economy, making it easier for businesses to create jobs and assist the unemployed. However, Germany's economy was soon struggling through the very early stages of what would come to be known in 2009 as the Eurozone crisis, a period of economic hardship that affected all countries using the **euro**. The crisis called for a shift in priorities to provide immediate help to German citizens struggling to make ends meet. She was praised in 2010 for extending what Germans call *Kurzarbeit*, or short-time work, to 2012. This government program implemented by the Federal Employment Agency helped ease unemployment by helping pay over half of an employee's salary when hours or wages had to be cut. The Federal Employment Agency also completely covered employees' pensions and healthcare.

Throughout the Eurozone crisis, Merkel always kept her support for working Germans at the forefront of her administration's agenda. They deserve the government's help because, as Merkel has said,

"The workers aren't responsible for this crisis."

A struggling European economy wasn't the only problem Merkel faced during her first term. Climate change brought on by increasing human emissions of greenhouse gases threatened to dramatically alter the world's climate. In 2007, Merkel led the G8 Summit. The yearly meeting focuses on global issues and includes eight powerful countries: Canada, France, Germany, Italy, Japan, Russia, the United Kingdom, and the U.S. During the 2007 summit, the participating countries agreed to consider cutting greenhouse gas emissions in half by 2050. Although the agreement drew criticism for being too leisurely an approach to something that needed immediate action, the summit helped to draw attention to the issue.

Working with Her Opponents: Second Term

After weathering four years of sink-or-swim experience in the international spotlight, what did Merkel think of politics before her second term began in 2009? In Merkel's own words,

> *"[I enjoy] not knowing in the morning what will happen in the evening. The fact that events are constantly confronting you with new situations. You meet new people all the time, and I'm very interested in people."*

Merkel often had to work with many different kinds of people, including those who did not share her political vision. When Merkel began her second term in 2009, she had to deal with a new coalition consisting of her CDU and sister CSU parties, along with the pro-business Free Democratic Party, which had a better showing than usual in the 2009 election. As it often happens in politics, alliances are seemingly forged between those who at first glance seem at odds over an issue. This was the case with Free Democratic Party leader Guido Westerwelle.

Despite their coalition agreement, Westerwelle accused Merkel of not having a plan laid out for her time in office, saying she lacked strategy and foresight. When asked whether she really wanted to work with the person who said such things, Merkel confirmed that indeed she did. She pointed to the bigger picture: what the coalition in Parliament could accomplish for Germany. Her approach impressed Westerwelle, who would go on to work closely with her from 2009 to 2013 in his capacities as Free Democratic Party chair,

Guido Westerwelle was head of the Free Democratic Party in 2013. He and Merkel worked together closely on foreign affairs, despite Westerwelle's initial public criticism.

Vice-Chancellor, and Minister of Foreign Affairs. Although he has since stepped down from all of these roles, he and Merkel remain close. She continues to turn to him to explain what is going on in his party, trusting him over his successor, Philipp Rösler.

Facing Controversy

While critics may rail against politicians, they don't necessarily understand what it's like to live in the spotlight, or actually be responsible for policies that affect millions of people. When you are charged with that responsibility, you undoubtedly learn to choose battles and develop a thicker skin. For her part, Angela Merkel was not afraid to work with—and sometimes even praise—those who had different or controversial beliefs, quoting former German chancellor Konrad Adenour: "If two people always have the same opinion, neither are worth anything." She does not censor her critics when they question her. Instead, she strives to protect their democratic right to express their opinion.

An example of this is how Merkel handled the public's mixed reaction of the award she presented to editorial cartoonist Kurt Westergaard. In 2005, Danish newspaper *Jyllands-Posten* published an editorial cartoon he had done which featured the Muslim prophet Muhammad. The cartoon was also republished in other countries' newspapers, including Germany, which borders Denmark. While some of the simultaneously published cartoon illustrations the newspapers ran were peaceful, Westergaard's depicted or alluded to a violent Muhammad with a bomb in his turban. Many Muslims believe that images of Muhammad should not ever be made, and many took offense at the violent depiction. Westergaard's cartoons in particular offended members of the Islamic worldwide community, and some Muslims protested the depiction, some rioted, and a few threatened violence.

The rift brought up several issues, the most prominent being freedom of speech, respect for religious values, and integration of cultures. Angela Merkel was particularly

Muslims protest a cartoon of Muhammad outside the Danish embassy in Berlin. The left sign demands that the EU prevent "xenophobia," or hatred of strangers. Merkel lauded the cartoonist's "courage."

sensitive and understanding of those issues having grown up in East Germany, whose dictatorship prohibited free speech, and whose leaders tried to manipulate the Christian religious community to further their own political agenda.

The event and resulting reactions were complex. Reminding attendees of the dictatorship that ended only twenty years before, and pointing out that it would have censored and possibly punished him for expressing himself, Merkel presented Kurt Westergaard with an award in 2010, saying,

> *"The secret of freedom is courage."*

At the same ceremony where she celebrated the freedom to express what could seem offensive, she also admonished a U.S. citizen who had announced his plans to burn a copy of the Quran, Islam's holy text. She called the act "repugnant, and simply wrong."

Merkel and the Question of a Diverse Germany

In 2010, while speaking to the Christian Democratic Union, Angela Merkel claimed that multiculturalism had failed in Germany, and that different cultures were unable to live together there. At the time, the country was almost 20 percent non-native German, and many hailed from Turkey. The issue was complicated further by Merkel's continued resistance to allowing Turkey to join the European Union (in 2013, Germany refused to continue talking to the country about its potential as an European Union **member state**), and by the fact that most Turkish people practice the Muslim faith.

She spoke publically about her Christian affiliation around this time, saying, "I am a member of the evangelical church. I believe in God and religion is also my constant companion… We as Christians should above all not be afraid of standing up for our beliefs." Up until this point in her political career, Chancellor Merkel had refrained from speaking publically about her religious affiliation. She erred in the eyes of many when she went on to claim in this speech that Christianity was the most persecuted religion.

Many people applied political motives to Merkel's pronouncement, claiming that she was disparaging German Muslims or trying to appeal to conservative CDU members. While she stressed the importance of separation of church and state in Germany as a democratic nation, Merkel also said the country was not built secularly (without religion), nor should it be.

Religious freedom, legislation, and history were also tangled in 2012 when Angela Merkel helped make it legal to circumcise infant boys, a religious rite practiced by many Jews, Muslims, Christians, and others. Opponents, including judges, argued that the act caused bodily harm. The matter was complicated further because of Germany's history of persecution of religions, most notably the Holocaust. Merkel may have felt compelled to avoid the appearance of impropriety in this case just as strongly as she felt it was a matter of religious freedom.

Fukushima Disaster

A nuclear disaster occurred in Japan in March 2011 during Merkel's second term as chancellor. An earthquake caused a tsunami that hit nuclear reactors at the Fukushima Daiichi nuclear plant. The waves caused flooding that ruined the power systems. Three nuclear reactors melted down because they could not be cooled. Radiation, a byproduct of nuclear power that can cause cancer in those who are exposed to it, poured out and contaminated the air, ground, and sea water.

Merkel had had a vested interest in nuclear power's viability. Before her political career, she was a physicist who wholly supported nuclear power, which is a popular source of energy, especially in Europe. As Germany's Federal Minister for the Environment, Nature Conservation, and Nuclear Safety in 1994, she had had to consider safety, security, and affordability when considering an energy source's pros and cons. To many, nuclear energy seemed to balance all of these factors better than other forms of energy production. Merkel hadn't previously considered that such an event could occur in such a tech-savvy country, but the Fukushima meltdown proved just how fragile and dangerous this energy can be.

Merkel did a 180-degree turn after Fukushima, declaring that Germany would stop using nuclear power plants by 2022. It was a seemingly simple proclamation to make, but it is, as most everything in politics, a complicated, multilayered topic. Perspectives vary, from German citizens, who worry about paying for potentially more expensive energy sources, to legislators who have to reconcile existing laws and provisions, to current energy providers who employ vast numbers of people.

An earthquake and tsunami resulted in a toxic meltdown at Japan's Fukushima Daiichi power plant in 2011. The environmental disaster prompted Merkel to reassess her energy policy.

The time of the nuclear meltdown proved to be an especially difficult time for Merkel. In addition to monitoring that situation and juggling the Eurozone crisis, Merkel's father, Horst Kasner, passed away in September 2011.

Third Term: 2013

For the first time in years, the unemployment rate in Germany was finally manageable in 2013, and the federal budget was headed in the right direction. Now entering her third term, Chancellor Merkel and her grand coalition were expected to focus on the *autobahn* (highway), education, state-funded childcare, pension increases, and a financial reorganization between the *Länder* and federal governments. As she had done before, Merkel sought to balance the budget, which had a deficit, by 2016.

In addition to tackling these issues, Merkel and her party members were committed to continually working on the Eurozone crisis, and addressing the climate change issue. Merkel also committed Germany to following the *Energiewende*, or "energy transition," course. The program focuses on forgoing nonrenewable energy reliance, such

Christian Democratic Union members applaud chairperson Angela Merkel in 2013. The CDU kept its lead but had to form a new coalition after the election.

as coal and other fossil fuels, in favor of switching to renewable resources, such as wind and solar power. With the lessons learned from the Fukushima disaster, Merkel herself said she would like to completely move Germany's coal and nuclear energy dependency to renewable energy sources during her third term.

NSA Wiretap Controversy: German–U.S. Relations

Germany's relations with the U.S. became rocky in 2013 when it was leaked that the U.S.'s National Security Agency (NSA), in an effort to prevent possible terrorist attacks, was spying on some of its political allies, including those in Germany. Even Merkel's own private cellphone was the target of a wiretap.

Though familiar with the kind of surveillance utilized by the Stasi in communist Germany, Merkel publicly refused to draw connections. She hesitated to imagine what the Stasi would be capable of with current technology, and said that the comparison diminishes what the Stasi actually did in the past. She acknowledged that there was a balance between protecting personal information and protecting a country. However, she wanted to learn what was true and what was rumor about the NSA spying reports, and has since been talking with the U.S. about the extent and means of surveillance. Despite the breach in trust, Merkel tried not to let the incident affect the relationship between the two countries, saying,

> *"We need trust among allies and partners. Such trust now has to be built anew."*

The Chancellor and the Saucepan: Merkel's Personal Life

At a glance, Angela Merkel seems all business, comfortable with the power of her position. She is chancellor of Germany and a major European Union leader. Famously hard working, she is known to start texting before breakfast in the morning. She often digs in her purse for her "handy" (her phone) during Bundestag sessions to keep abreast of her seemingly never-ending schedule of meetings, appearances, and conferences.

However, Merkel is not, nor should she be, defined only by her office. As she once said of herself,

> *"When I'm stirring a saucepan I don't say to myself, 'Now the chancellor is stirring a saucepan.'"*

Speaking of saucepans, Merkel enjoys cooking for friends and family, and does have particular food preferences. She prefers a thick, spicy, sour Russian soup called *solyanka*, as well as Hungarian stew. Both of the recipes were commonly served during her childhood in East Germany.

Merkel and U.S. President Barack Obama suffered strained relations after the revelation that the NSA spies on allies, including Germany.

Although Merkel is notoriously private, she sustains friendships and working relationships. Beate Baumann, for example, has been her private secretary and personal friend since the 1990s. No doubt Baumann has seen Merkel do her infamous impressions of former French president Nicolas Sarkozy and U.S. president Barack Obama. Merkel's dry sense of humor is occasionally let loose in public, too. When asked in an interview with a journalist from *Süddeutsche Zeitung* magazine whom she would invite to dinner if she could invite anyone in the world, Merkel at first deadpanned, "I don't give dinner parties." She capitulated by finally admitting she would eat with Vicente del Bosque, the coach of Spain's *futbol* (soccer) team. She is a big fan of the sport.

Time away from her role as chancellor is spent relaxing with her husband and friends. She and her husband

Hand Holding

Besides worrying about what voting blocs to appeal to and how much compromise is too much, many politicians are faced with a common problem: What should they do with their hands? Chancellor Merkel holds hers together in what is referred to as the "Merkel diamond," or "Merkel rhombus." Her gesture has become a common symbol in Germany. It's so familiar that during her most recent run for chancellor, a large Christian Democratic Union campaign billboard showed just her hands in the diamond shape. The accompanying slogan read, "Germany's future—in good hands."

Not everyone feels safe when they see the Merkel diamond, however. The CDU billboard was hit with plenty of negative feedback. Critics say the representation lacked substance, and that Merkel's following is really about a **cult of personality**. Frequent comparisons were also made between Merkel and Mr. Burns, the ruthless business owner in *The Simpsons*, a U.S. animated television show. In the show, Burns holds his hands in a similar position as Merkel does.

Merkel addressed with mock seriousness the question of why she posed with her hands together in this fashion: as a trained scientist, she simply solved a "practical problem."

travel to Tyrol and to Ischia, an Italian island, for vacations. (Photos of those trips are rare, because German politicians are generally given more privacy than those in the U.S.) She still loves art and reading as much as she did when she was growing up, and her favorite movie is *The Legend of Paul and Paula*, considered by many to be an East German classic. Finally, she is perhaps most famously an opera fan. She and her husband attend the Bayreuth Festival every year to enjoy Richard Wagner's operas—*Tristan and Isolde* is a favorite.

Merkel attended a 2008 opera house opening in Norway's capital of Oslo. When the media opined on her dress, Merkel replied they reacted that way solely because she is a woman.

CHAPTER FIVE

The Legacy of the Most Powerful Woman in the World

"The most powerful politician in Europe" and "the world's most powerful woman" are titles commonly applied to Angela Merkel—and not without reason. *Forbes* magazine named her the second most powerful person in the world in 2012, after U.S. President Barack Obama. Germans refer to her as a *Machtfrau*, "woman of power," but Merkel says, "Power is relative in Germany's political system." She has also explained that, "Everything is based on the power to convince others. I have to constantly convince citizens, my party, and my coalition partners."

Merkel's powers of persuasion were put to the test following the financial crash of several European Union countries. Because Germany was doing so well financially, Merkel held most the authority when

Greece's economy was the first domino to fall in 2010 in the wake of this global economic crisis.

Why is Germany helping Greece and the rest of the affected countries, including Portugal, Italy, Ireland, and Spain? And how does that relate to her position of most powerful woman in the world?

The European Union

Belgium, Denmark, France, Germany, Greece, Ireland, Italy, Luxembourg, the Netherlands, Portugal, Spain, and the United Kingdom were the original member states of the European Union (EU), a political and economic confederation of several European countries. The Maastricht Treaty created the European Union in 1992, when Angela Merkel was beginning her political career. Officially known as the Treaty of the European Union, the Maastricht Treaty replaces 1957's European Economic Community and increases the European Parliament's power. Participating countries are known as member states and share a common cultural and legislative core.

Angela Merkel has been an outspoken supporter of the EU's goals, saying, "Above all it is important to point out that we can only maintain our prosperity in Europe if we belong to the most innovative regions in the world…"

The Maastricht Treaty granted European Union citizenship to those people living in the member states, which allows them to live in any of the participating countries. Regardless of what country they reside in, they are assured the right to vote in both continent-wide and local elections. Voting rights are considered so important that in 2013, the **European Commission** cracked down on Bulgaria for requiring non-Bulgarians to provide more than the standard proof to vote. The legal action was dropped after Bulgaria changed its policy.

The EU has three parts: the **European Community**, the Common Foreign and Security Policy, and Justice and Home Affairs. The European Community houses the European Coal and Steel Community, which initiated the organization in 1950. The European Community is also home to Euratom, the European Atomic Energy Community, which is responsible for managing member states' nuclear power use.

This 2005 European Union map shows current member states in white. Candidate member states are named and in tan.

Countries continue to express interest in joining the European Union, and are split into two categories: candidates and potential candidates. Candidates are currently applying EU law nationally. Potential candidates haven't yet fulfilled the organization's requirements for joining. As of December 2013, the EU is more than twice as big as when it started, with twenty-eight member states. In addition to its own currency, the euro, the EU has its own holiday, flag, anthem, and motto: "United in diversity."

Angela Merkel likes the EU's direction and is interested in further "political union, because Europe needs to forge its own unique path. We need to become incrementally closer and closer, in all policy areas... Over a long process, we will transfer more powers to the [European] Commission, which will then handle what falls within its areas like a government of Europe."

The European Union won the Nobel Peace Prize in 2012. The Nobel committee cited the EU's peace efforts over the past decades, saying that their unity efforts helped turn a divisive continent into a unified one. At the time it received the award, several EU member states were nearing economic ruin. Vast efforts to keep them afloat were at times met with thousands of protesting citizens. Nobel committee head Thorbjørn Jagland warned that if the EU crumbled, the past peace efforts might be for naught: "The stabilising part played by the EU has helped to transform most of Europe from a continent of war to a continent of peace." German chancellor Angela Merkel was touched by the award, and recognized it as a reason to continue trying to keep the EU afloat.

A Continent in Trouble

The Eurozone crisis started in 2009 when Greece suffered an economic crash, putting the other members of the European Union at risk of financial ruin. A number of factors contributed to this dire economic state, including careless spending, borrowing, lending, unheeded finance reforms, and inaccurate accounting on the part of all countries involved.

By most accounts, the roots of this crisis lie in Greece, which for years had been spending far more than it was collecting in taxes, and had been underreporting their national budget deficit to the European Union. The EU has a national debt limit of 60 percent of a country's **gross domestic product**, or GDP. Greece revealed in December 2009 that its national debt was more than twice the EU's limit—higher than any other country in modern history. When word got out that the country could no longer sustain its huge debt, the country "defaulted," meaning it could no longer take out loans to cover its bills.

With Greece unable to fulfill its economic obligations, the crisis spread to other countries in the Eurozone with struggling economies—Italy, Ireland, Portugal, Spain, and Cyprus—each falling over like dominoes in a line. The United States, the world's largest

The Euro

The euro, the EU's common currency, is another effort to promote unity and stability and facilitate economic transactions among member states. As chancellor, Angela Merkel's belief in the euro and its unifying ability has been steadfast. She maintained that, "If the euro fails, then Europe and the idea of European union will fail."

Before the introduction of the euro, each European country had its own currency: the *Deutschmark* in Germany, the *franc* in France, the *lira* in Italy, and so on. Before foreign visitors to a country could purchase something, they would first have to convert their money to that country's currency. Given the proximity of European countries, these exchanges were common. However, because the comparative value of these currencies, called exchange rates, varied across countries, currency conversions were extremely complicated. In 1979, France and Germany instigated the start of the European Monetary System, where many European countries linked their currencies to prevent large exchange rate fluctuations. Although the initiative helped with the problem of currency exchange rates between European countries, the ongoing need to physically exchange the different types of currency was still problematic for travelers.

The Hanover European Council's appointed committee submitted a report in April of 1989 (just months before the Berlin Wall fell) asserting that the EU's goal of economic accord between member states would be more easily met if it followed three main steps: allowing currency to move freely, combining member states' monetary policies and cooperating among national banks, and using a single denomination as the accepted currency. This currency was called the euro. The European Central Bank, which is independent of any one member state, was created to work with the national banks from each participating member state to ensure the stability of this new money.

In 2014, the euro is still the only accepted currency in most existing and candidate member states of the EU. It makes commerce easier, and it financially binds the participating member states together. However, when one member state is in financial jeopardy, all of them are. That is why the financial crisis that started in Greece in 2009 spread its way to other EU countries, and why Angela Merkel had to try to lead the countries out of it. Drawing from her childhood spent in a country that was split, and the powerful support she received for her chancellorship in Germany and in other EU member states, she became the person most likely to help keep the European Union together.

economy, was also going through its own economic downturn—the Great **Recession**—that complicated things even further throughout the rest of the world.

The Eurozone crisis threatened to ruin the economies of many EU member nations. Widespread unemployment and fewer purchases have been the result. Interest rates on loans have gone up to help prevent inflation, leaving the defaulting countries with less and less money to repay their debts. This cycle has proven hard to break.

Later, the collapsed countries would have banks' lending policies to blame as well. Bonds, which are borrowed money from the public that is paid back with interest, help fund banks and companies. Banks had declared that all member states' bonds were equal when the countries accepted the euro, which initially helped make the euro work. When the economic slump hit, these same banks, as well as corporations, citizens, and governments, were suffering.

Failure to solve the problem could lead to more than the collapse of the European Union. It could also result in widespread mistrust between the member states that have invested so much in each others' success, only to lose it all. Merkel described the situation as being on the "brink of a precipice," with everything the EU had built about to topple over.

Since the Eurozone crisis and the collapse of several economies, many European countries have turned specifically to Germany for help. Although Germany had borrowed more than the EU allows during the reunification of its country, Germans have since buckled down and become expert exporters (especially to other EU member states). Because Germany's economy was so strong, and their budget was balanced in 2010 (thanks to Merkel), they were obligated to help the suffering countries. However, despite Germany's position to lead the Eurozone out of the crisis, Merkel warned,

> *"History gives us Europeans no such thing as a legal right to be a leading continent in the world. The severe crisis that we are currently going through in the Eurozone shows that Europe must learn, from the debt crisis, the right lessons..."*

Merkel's approach to the financial trouble, like most of her leadership, was often seen as the result of growing up in a place that lacked necessities—and ceased to exist partly because of it. She has expressed empathy with those Europeans affected by the crisis, saying, "I come from a country that experienced economic collapse."

Solving the Eurozone Crisis

The European Union's common currency, culture, markets, and borders made for intense interest in each others' finances when the crisis was revealed. Since the population and GDP of both Germany and France were the highest in the EU, those countries were called to help Greece and the other floundering EU member states. **Austerity** is the word often used to describe Merkel's approach to the Eurozone crisis: restricted spending. Some described the approach as thrifty, but critics said it was harsh, citing raised taxes and a higher retirement age. The often-called "austerity measures" had already been implemented in Greece by its own government. However, despite these measures, Greece still couldn't straighten its course by itself, nor after a multibillion-euro loan from other EU member states and the International Monetary Fund.

When loans didn't help, Angela Merkel met with leaders from other euro-compliant EU member states in May 2010 and they created two entities: the European Financial Stability Facility and the European Financial Stabilisation Mechanism. The European Financial Stability Facility would come to be known as a temporary "bailout" plan that would be implemented over several years for some of the EU member states in crisis.

Merkel's past gave her a special purpose to pursue European unity. As she said,

"At German unification, we were lucky to get so much help from West Germany. Now, we have the good fortune of being able to help each other in Europe."

Merkel also communicated equally important sticking points. She was focused on saving Europe as a united group, and she believed that accountability and change should accompany the financial help; plans had to be sustainable with the long term in mind. She made it clear that the help came because she wants the EU to succeed, and that help should improve the situation, not complicate it.

The buck didn't stop with Merkel. European-backed loans have to be unanimously approved by EU member states. Any of the euro-compliant member states could have vetoed the move, but they didn't. Merkel's German parliament approved the European Financial Stability Facility expansion in September 2011. At the same time, they also created a Bundestag committee to oversee future parliamentary involvement in European Financial Stabilisation Mechanism decisions.

The temporary became permanent. The European Stability Mechanism replaced the European Financial Stability Facility in October 2012. More than half of German citizens didn't want to instate the European Stability Mechanism. Merkel's party, the Christian Democratic Union, wasn't enthusiastic about sharing the debt of the failing countries across the EU, or putting the responsibility on every country's shoulders. Merkel herself acknowledged that previous strategies alone, including austerity and loans, hadn't solved the crisis, but she continued supporting efforts that moved the euro-compliant member states under a single umbrella.

Together, Merkel and French president Nicolas Sarkozy convinced every member state except Britain and the Czech Republic to accept oversight from the EU. Instead of each member state creating its own budget, the EU would have oversight. If a country spent over its set limit, it would be forced to face penalties.

Merkel wanted accountability for mismanaged companies and banks, and that required financial unity among European nations. To attain this goal, she was willing to give more power to the EU than to her own country. She refused to budge when member countries asked for more time to repay loans. She also explained,

"Good politicians always have doubts, as a way of constantly reviewing whether they are on the right track."

By saying this, the German chancellor revealed what some perceived as a weakness in the midst of the struggle by admitting she wasn't sure her decisions were leading to her goals. Merkel was often criticized for her stoicism, but her humanity in this case was clearly in view.

European Union: Perceptions

Many Europeans, including some EU members, questioned Merkel's decisions. The austerity measures implemented in Greece sparked outrage. Riots and protests were common during the economic crisis and many were in direct opposition to the cutbacks—layoffs, lowered wages, higher taxes, frozen pensions—despite the fact that most of those had been initiated by the Greek government before the European Union bailout was given.

Merkel visited Athens, Greece, in October 2012 to talk with leaders about the nation's economic woes. Over 50,000 people were there to protest the EU budget requirements and their own government's measures. Some protestors claimed that Germany was asking too much of Greece's citizens. Others claimed that the EU-enforced cutbacks were causing a recession. (Experts actually disagree among themselves on this. Some economists believe austerity leads to recession, and that the way out of financial trouble is by introducing more money into the economy via tax rebates and low-interest loans.) While the majority of protesters were not violent, the violence that did occur was striking: burning tear gas bottles were thrown amid passionate screams for Merkel to leave.

Critics to Merkel's plans came in the form of politician and regular EU citizens alike. Merkel was "too slow," Merkel was "too severe," Merkel was "too sweeping," and many believed that she was not allowing the other EU leaders to have a voice in the decision-making. In actuality, her decisions were often made with the input and support of other EU leaders. Merkel also had to lead her own country at the same time she was trying to help revive the economies of Greece, Portugal, Italy, Ireland, and Spain. Her efforts were on maintaining (and eventually deepening) unity, and she knew that further EU economic crisis could lead to trouble for Germany, too.

Angela Merkel was aware that many people were suffering. She urged employers to hire people, especially young people, with whom Merkel empathized. She said she wanted them to know that she was aware of what it was like for them, having faced similar conditions while growing up in East Germany.

While the German chancellor had no shortage of critics, she had champions as well. Poland's Foreign Minister Radek Sikorski said of Merkel's job, "nobody else can do it," by which he meant solve the economic crisis. From the beginning of the crisis, Merkel worked directly with French president Nicolas Sarkozy, who said, "I admire Madame Merkel. She runs her country well."

Merkel saw the situation not just as a crisis but also an opportunity: "We have a common currency, but no common political and economic union… and this is exactly what we must change. To achieve this—therein lies the opportunity of the crisis." That opportunity made some Europeans nervous. Some were concerned she would leave behind or exclude member states, such as Britain, that opted out of reforms. Others, reminded of World War II, were scared that Germany was becoming too powerful again. Credit risk advisor Nicholas Spiro said this about Merkel and Germany: "No other leader of a major economy has been able to reap more political dividends from an international financial and economic crisis." The country had invested deeply in the banks in Greece, Spain, and Ireland—all countries it helped bail out of the economic crisis. The takeover fears went so deep that they culminated in some critics directly comparing Angela Merkel to Adolf Hitler.

Merkel's Legacy and the EU's Future

To date, the Eurozone crisis remains Merkel's messiest and most difficult challenge as chancellor. However, helping to solve that crisis will most likely be remembered as the most important accomplishment—or failure— of Angela Merkel's chancellorship. So far, signs are good: Germans, who have had to assume a significant responsibility for helping other European Union member nations recover from the crisis, reelected Merkel for a third term in December 2013. In the midst of difficult economic and political reforms, her reelection was a hearty literal vote of confidence in her abilities to handle the situation.

An EU summit to be held in Brussels in June 2014 is planned to discuss the continuing crisis. Decisions made there could change the European Union and the euro forever. Merkel's plan requires euro-compliant member states to sign a contract that limits their spending, cuts public debt, and reforms elements like pension age and wages. The European Commission would enforce the contract deadlines, and violating member states would be fined.

Despite her proposal being unpopular, Merkel has insisted that the European court of justice watch public spending and budget policies in the euro-compliant member states. She also wants to create a single European political organization to oversee member states, a more powerful European parliament, and European court of justice power over Europe's supreme court. Merkel understands that foundational changes like those would take years, suggesting they come "sometime in the future, as I say, and after a goodly number of interim stages."

Her reelection led to new coalitions within German government, however. Merkel has had to work with more fiscally liberal parties—the Social Democratic Party in particular. Member states operating under economic reforms hoped for less austerity from Merkel as a result of these new coalitions in 2013.

Merkel will continue working with France's current president, François Hollande, who wants Merkel to focus less on her domestic German matters and more on the EU. He has pressured Merkel to assure Greece that it can continue using the euro. Hollande has also tried getting Merkel to bend on accepting bonds and austerity measures, urging her to lower taxes and raise wages.

Despite these pressures, Merkel remains firm in her vision for a financially stable Eurozone. Merkel participated in twenty-six hours of negotiation with EU leaders to agree upon the Multiannual Financial Framework, limiting how much and on what the EU can spend money. Her four-year chancellorship, the 2016 Multiannual Financial Framework assessment, and the 2014 summit could converge to create a new European Union, one prepared to solve its current issues while also looking ahead to tackle whatever challenges may come next. As Angela Merkel has said, "I don't want the EU to be a museum for all the things that used to be good. I want an EU which successfully strives to create new things."

From left: Andrea Nahles (Minister of Work and Social Issues), Horst Seehofer (CSU chair), Merkel, Sigmar Gabriel (SPD chair), and Hermann Gröhe (Minister of Health) celebrate a 2013 coalition agreement.

Timeline

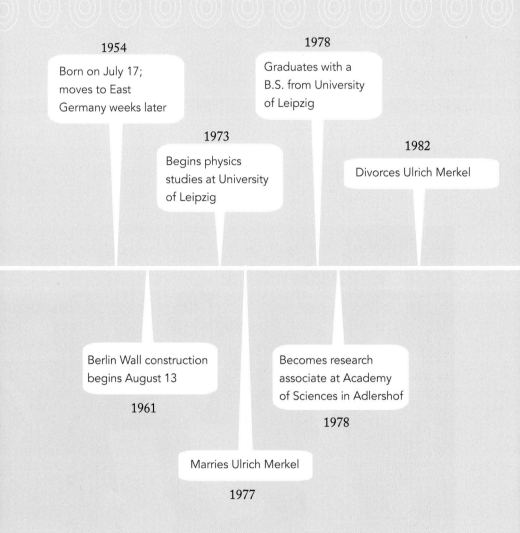

1954
Born on July 17; moves to East Germany weeks later

1973
Begins physics studies at University of Leipzig

1978
Graduates with a B.S. from University of Leipzig

1982
Divorces Ulrich Merkel

Berlin Wall construction begins August 13
1961

Becomes research associate at Academy of Sciences in Adlershof
1978

Marries Ulrich Merkel
1977

1986

Graduates with a
PhD from German
Academy of Sciences

2005

Elected chancellor
of Germany

2011

In March, Fukushima
Daiichi nuclear disaster
scatters toxic radiation
across a large portion
of Japan; September 2,
Merkel's father dies

1990

Elected to Bundestag

Berlin Wall comes down
on November 9

1989

Reelected chancellor
of Germany; Eurozone
crisis begins in Greece,
threatening the economies
of many European countries

2009

Marries Dr. Joachim Sauer

1998

Reelected chancellor
of Germany

2013

SOURCE NOTES

Chapter 1

P. 5, Jordans, Frank, "How Angela Merkel Went from Marching with Communist Youth to Germany's First Female Chancellor," http://news.nationalpost.com/2013/09/20/how-angela-merkel-went-from-marching-with-communist-youth-to-germanys-first-female-chancellor/.

P. 8, Dempsey, Judy, "The Young Merkel: Idealist's Daughter," http://www.nytimes.com/2005/09/05/world/europe/05iht-germany.html?pagewanted=all&_r=0.

P. 9, Eddy, Melissa, "Merkel Offers a Peek Into Her Private Life," http://www.nytimes.com/2013/05/18/world/europe/fascination-with-german-leaders-more-private-side.html?_r=1&.

P. 10, Dempsey, "The Young Merkel: Idealist's Daughter."

Pp. 10-11, Marx, Karl. *Introduction to a Contribution to the Critique of Hegel's Philosophy of Right*. (New York, NY: Oxford University Press, 1970), p.3.

P. 11, Tiffen, Stuart, "Merkel's Father, a Clergyman Under Communism, Dies Aged 85," http://www.dw.de/merkels-father-a-clergyman-under-communism-dies-aged-85/a-15362772.

P. 11, Dempsey, "The Young Merkel: Idealist's Daughter."

P. 13, Crawford, Alan and Tony Czuczka, "Angela Merkel's Years in East Germany Shaped Her Crisis Politics," http://www.businessweek.com/articles/2013-09-19/angela-merkels-early-years-in-east-germany-shaped-her-crisis-politics.

P. 13, Smale, Alison, "The Making of Angela Merkel," http://rendezvous.blogs.nytimes.com/2012/10/30/the-making-of-angela-merkel/.

P. 13, Smale, Alison, "The Making of Angela Merkel."

P. 14, Berlin Wall Memorial, "The Border Fortifications in the Eighties," http://www.berliner-mauer-gedenkstaette.de/en/aufbau-der-grenzanlagen-49.html.

P. 14, Berlin Wall Memorial, "The Border Fortifications in the Eighties."

P. 15, Berlin Wall Memorial, "Expanding the Wall, 1961 to 1989," http://www.berliner-mauer-gedenkstaette.de/en/grenzausbau-47.html.

P. 16, "Stasi Order to Shoot at Escapers Found," http://usatoday30.usatoday.com/news/topstories/2007-08-11-2657715740_x.htm.

P. 16, Miller, Dorothy, "Report: The Food Situation in East Germany," http://osaarchivum.org/files/holdings/300/8/3/text/24-5-79.shtml.

Pp. 16–17, Smale, Alison, "The Making of Angela Merkel."

P. 17, "Chancellor Recalls Communist Childhood: Merkel Admits She Still Tends to Stockpile," http://www.spiegel.de/international/germany/chancellor-recalls-communist-childhood-merkel-admits-she-still-tends-to-stockpile-a-719754.html.

P. 17, Alexander, Von Robin and Jochen Gaugele, "Habe über eine Ausreise aus der DDR nachgedacht," http://www.welt.de/politik/deutschland/article118233586/Habe-ueber-eine-Ausreise-aus-der-DDR-nachgedacht.html.

P. 17, Alexander and Gaugele, "Habe über eine Ausreise aus der DDR nachgedacht."

P. 19, Alexander and Gaugele, "Habe über eine Ausreise aus der DDR nachgedacht."

P. 19, Marr, Andrew, *The Making of Angela Merkel, a German Enigma*. London: BBC News, 2013. Television documentary.

P. 19, Crawford and Czuczka, "Angela Merkel's Years in East Germany Shaped Her Crisis Politics."

P. 20, "New Biography Causes Stir: How Close Was Merkel to the Communist System?" Spiegel Online International, http://www.spiegel.de/international/germany/new-book-suggests-angela-merkel-was-closer-to-communism-than-thought-a-899768.html.

Chapter 2

P. 24, Merkel, Angela, "Speech by the Chancellor at the 5th Meeting of 11 Synod of the EKD," http://www.ekd.de/synode2012/grussworte/grusswort_merkel.html.

P. 25, Köttker, Verena, "Interview mit Ulrich Merkel," http://www.focus.de/schlagwoerter/personen/u/ulrich-merkel/.

P. 27, Kornelius, Stefan. *Angela Merkel: The Chancellor and Her World* (Kindle Edition) (Richmond, United Kingdom: Alma Books Ltd., 2013).

P. 27, Peel, Quentin, "Angela Merkel: A Woman of Power," http://www.ft.com/intl/cms/s/2/347c8b84-44b2-11e2-8fd7-00144feabdc0.html#axzz2tstqjtTV.

P. 28, Merkel, Angela, "Speech by Federal Chancellor Angela Merkel at the opening ceremony of the 61st academic year of the College of Europe in Bruges, November 2, 2010," https://www.coleurope.eu/

content/news/Speeches/Europakolleg%20Brugge%20
Mitschrift%20englisch.pdf.

Pp. 28–29, Quinn, Susan, *Marie Curie: A Life.* (New York
City New York: Simon and Schuster, 1995), p. 48

P. 30, Kirschbaum, Erik, "Special Report: Don't Call Him
Mr. Merkel," Reuters, May 16, 2012, http://www.reu-
ters.com/article/2012/05/16/us-germany-sauer-idUS-
BRE84F07420120516.

P. 33, Angela Merkel, "Persönlich," http://www.ange-
la-merkel.de/persönlich.html.

P. 35, "Ein Gespräch mit Angela Merkel," http://www.
brigitte.de/frauen/politik/angela-merkel-inter-
view-540566/.

Chapter 3

P. 37, Peel, "Angela Merkel: A Woman of Power."

P. 38, Marr, *The Making of Angela Merkel, a German Enigma.*

P. 39, Merkel, "Persönlich."

P. 43, Merkel, Angela, "Die von Helmut Kohl eingeräumten
Vorgänge haben der Partei Schaden zugefügt," http://
germanhistorydocs.ghi-dc.org/docpage.cfm?docpage_
id=4595&language=english.

Pp. 43–44, Merkel, Angela, "Die von Helmut Kohl

eingeräumten Vorgänge haben der Partei Schaden zugefügt."

P. 44, Dempsey, "The Young Merkel: Idealist's Daughter."

P. 46, Miller, Nick, "The Mother Land: How Germany Fell in Love with Angela Merkel," http://www.smh.com.au/world/the-mother-land-how-germany-fell-in-love-with-angela-merkel-20130927-2ujk3.html#ixzz2p-B0ex1nv.

P. 47, Peel, "Angela Merkel: A Woman of Power."

P. 47, Marr, *The Making of Angela Merkel, a German Enigma.*

P. 47, *Marr, The Making of Angela Merkel, a German Enigma.*

P. 47, Marr, *The Making of Angela Merkel, a German Enigma.*

P. 48, , Mattel, Inc., "Barbie Presents Unique Angela Merkel Barbie Doll," http://investor.shareholder.com/mattel/releasedetail.cfm?ReleaseID=365110.

P. 50, "Merkel sieht viele Alternativen zur Frauenquote," http://www.wsj.de/article/SB100014241278873242669 04578462392507865154.html.

Chapter 4

P. 55, Moore, Tristana, "Merkel Saves Opel From GM's Fate," http://content.time.com/time/business/article/0,8599,1902163,00.html.

P. 56, Peel, "Angela Merkel: A Woman of Power."

P. 58, "Merkel Celebrates Coalition Deal with Social Democrats," http://www.euronews.com/2013/12/16/merkel-celebrates-coalition-deal-with-social-democrats/.

P. 60, "Award for Danish Muhammad Cartoonist: Merkel Defends Press Freedom, Condemns Koran-Burning," http://www.spiegel.de/international/germany/award-for-danish-muhammad-cartoonist-merkel-defends-press-freedom-condemns-koran-burning-a-716503.html.

P. 60, "Award for Danish Muhammad Cartoonist: Merkel Defends Press Freedom, Condemns Koran-Burning."

Pp. 60–61, Hall, Allan, "Germany's Iron Lady Angela Merkel Reveals she Believes in God—and Religion Has Always Been Her Constant Companion," http://www.dailymail.co.uk/news/article-2228664/Angela-Merkel-believes-God-strong-Christian-beliefs.html.

P. 66, Traynor, Ian, "Germany and France Warn NSA Spying Fallout Jeopardises Fight Against Terror," http://www.theguardian.com/world/2013/oct/25/germany-france-nsa-spying-merkel-hollande-eu.

P. 66, "A Safe Pair of Hands," http://www.economist.com/news/briefing/21586299-perceptions-germanys-chancellor-who-likely-win-re-election-september-22nd-are.

P. 67, "A Safe Pair of Hands."

P. 68, Jordans, "How Angela Merkel Went from Marching with Communist Youth to Germany's First Female Chancellor."

P. 68, "A Safe Pair of Hands."

P. 68, Jordans, "How Angela Merkel Went from Marching with Communist Youth to Germany's First Female Chancellor."

P. 68, Smale, "The Making of Angela Merkel."

Chapter 5

P. 71, "Angie Abroad: What Merkel's Win Means for Berlin's Allies," http://www.spiegel.de/international/world/what-does-merkel-s-win-mean-for-france-turkey-the-uk-and-russia-a-924222.html.

P. 71, "Howard, Caroline, "The World's Most Powerful Women 2013," http://www.forbes.com/power-women/.

P. 71, "Peel, "Angela Merkel: A Woman of Power."

P. 71, "Peel, "Angela Merkel: A Woman of Power."

P. 72, "Benoit, Bertrand and Andrew Gowers, "Transcript of Angela Merkel interview," http://www.ft.com/intl/cms/s/0/1291fe90-ebf5-11df-b50f-00144feab49a.html#axzz2tstqjtTV.

P. 74, "The history of the European Union," http://europa.
eu/about-eu/eu-history/index_en.htm.

P. 74, Traynor, Ian, "Angela Merkel casts doubt on
saving Greece from financial meltdown," http://
www.theguardian.com/world/2012/jan/25/ange-
la-merkel-greece-financial-meltdown.

Pp. 74-75, Harding, Luke, "European Union Wins Nobel
Peace Prize," http://www.theguardian.com/world/2012/
oct/12/european-union-nobel-peace-prize

P. 76, "Merkel Warns of Europe's Collapse: 'If Euro Fails,
So Will the Idea of European Union,'" http://www.
spiegel.de/international/germany/merkel-warns-of-eu-
rope-s-collapse-if-euro-fails-so-will-the-idea-of-euro-
pean-union-a-694696.html.

P. 78, Merkel, "Speech by Federal Chancellor Angela
Merkel at the Opening Ceremony of the 61st Academic Year of the College of Europe in Bruges, November
2, 2010."

P. 79, di Lorenzo, Giovanni and Tina Hildebrandt, "Ich bin
mit mir zufrieden," http://www.zeit.de/2013/29/ange-
la-merkel-interview.

P. 79, Crawford and Czuczka, "Angela Merkel's Years in
East Germany Shaped Her Crisis Politics."

P. 80, "Q&A: Greece's Financial Crisis Explained," http://www.cnn.com/2010/BUSINESS/02/10/greek.debt.qanda/.

P. 80, Greeley, Brendan, "Is Germany Responsible for the Euro Crisis?" http://www.businessweek.com/articles/2013-09-12/is-germany-responsible-for-the-euro-crisis.

P. 80, Crawford and Czuczka, "Angela Merkel's Years in East Germany Shaped Her Crisis Politics."

P. 82, Traynor, Ian, "Angela Merkel Casts Doubt on Saving Greece from Financial Meltdown," http://www.theguardian.com/world/2012/jan/25/angela-merkel-greece-financial-meltdown.

P. 83, Guild, Monty and Tony Danaher, "German Elections Endorse Merkel's Eurozone Recovery," http://www.financialsense.com/contributors/guild/german-elections-endorse-merkel-s-eurozone-recovery.

P. 83, "Merkel's Rival Steinbrueck Says Euro Zone Austerity too Severe," http://www.reuters.com/article/2012/12/30/us-eurozone-steinbrueck-idUSBRE8BT06120121230.

P. 83, Pauly, Christoph and Christoph Schult, "*Auf Wiedersehen* Austerity? Europe Hopes for Gentler Merkel," http://www.spiegel.de/international/europe/merkel-coalition-prospects-could-mean-softening-of-europe-policy-a-924176.html.

P. 84, Moulson, Geir, "Germany: Economic Giant Reluctant to Lead," http://bigstory.ap.org/article/germany-economic-giant-reluctant-lead.

P. 84, Willsher, Kim, "The Merkozys, Europe's Odd Couple, Announce Their Political Engagement," http://www.theguardian.com/world/2012/feb/06/merkozy-nicolas-sarkozy-angela-merkel.

P. 84, "Merkel Warns of Europe's Collapse: 'If Euro Fails, so Will the Idea of European Union.'"

P. 85, Walker, Andrew, "Concern in Greece Over Angela Merkel's Win," http://www.bbc.co.uk/news/business-24201522.

P. 86, Traynor, "Angela Merkel Casts Doubt on Saving Greece from Financial Meltdown."

P. 87, Traynor, Ian. "Angela Merkel Discovers Her Inner European," http://www.theguardian.com/world/2012/jan/25/angela-merkel-discovers-inner-european.

GLOSSARY

austerity Restricted spending. The approach Merkel used most during the Eurozone crisis.

Bundesrat The so-called upper house of the German Parliament. Holds representatives from the German *Länder*.

Bundestag The so-called lower house of the German Parliament. Holds nationally elected representatives.

capitalism An economic system based on individuals, instead of governments or groups of people, owning the means of production. Often thought of as the opposite of communism.

chancellor Head of German Parliament, elected by Bundestag, who governs by creating and passing laws for the country and the European Union. Officially, the third highest-ranking person in German government after parliamentary president and president (who has little power compared to the chancellor).

Christian Democratic Union (CDU) Conservative political party of which Angela Merkel is a member.

coalition Group of people or political parties that work together. In German politics, if the coalition is formed by the largest political parties, it is called a grand coalition.

communism An economic system based on all citizens working but sharing their resources equally. Can be democratic, but is often dictatorial. Commonly associated with socialism.

cult of personality When a large group of people are loyal, usually to a fault, to a person. It is implied that the person has cultivated that loyalty through various ways and mostly for personal gain.

defector A person who leaves a group or place, usually illegally or under suspicion.

Deutschland Germany. Formerly split into West and East Germany, but reunited into a single country in 1990 after communism's fall.

Deutschmark German form of currency created by World War II Allies U.S., Great Britain, and France.

euro International currency used by some European Union member states.

European Commission (EC) Works with European Union member states and acts as the EU executive body, introducing legislation to the European Parliament.

European Community (EC) One of three parts composing the European Union.

European Union (EU) A group of countries from the continent of Europe that have agreed to certain rules and common goals.

Eurozone crisis Financial emergency that occurred in European Union member states that employed the euro. Various causes contributed to the euro's downturn, which led to an economic recession in many member states and threatened to harm other EU nations.

Federal Republic of Germany (FRG) The capitalist democracy in West Germany before the German reunification in 1990.

Freie Deutsche Jugend **(FDJ)** East German youth organization that promoted socialism.

German Democratic Republic (GDR) The communist dictatorship in East Germany before the German reunification in 1990.

gross domestic product (GDP) Indicates, economically, how much a country is producing. It measures components like personal and government spending, expenses, and exports.

Länder German language for "states." There are sixteen total German states, and they elect members to the Bundesrat house in Parliament.

member state A country that is fully a part of the European Union. Member states may or may not use the euro as their currency.

parliament Democratic form of government. Germany's consists of the Bundestag and Bundesrat.

recession When an economy is not robust; unemployment is higher, wages are lower, and purchasing slows.

socialism An economic system often associated with communism in which government owns major factories and industries, and the welfare of citizens is taken care of as a group.

Stasi East German secret police force that spied on citizens from 1950 to 1990.

FURTHER INFORMATION

Books

Ellis, Deborah. *The Breadwinner*. Berkeley, CA: Ground-wood Books, 2000.

Schneider, Peter. *The Wall Jumper: A Berlin Story*. Chicago, IL: Pantheon Books, 1983.

Hensel, Jana. *After the Wall*. New York, NY: PublicAffairs, 2004.

Websites

Deutschland
www.deutschland.de/en
Germany's official website offers information from sports to history to education.

Energy Transition: The German Energiewende
energytransition.de/
Energiewende (Germany's energy transition away from nonrenewable resources) is explained here.

European Union
europa.eu/index_en.htm
Aspects of the European Union are explained here. Choose a country from the menu to find out specifically how the EU is a part of it.

SELECTED BIBLIOGRAPHY

Alessi, Christopher. "A New Fiscal Union for Europe."
Council on Foreign Relations, December 9, 2011.
http://www.cfr.org/world/new-fiscal-union-europe/
p26731.

"Angela Merkel: A Safe Pair of Hands." *The Economist*,
September 14, 2013. http://www.economist.com/news/
briefing/21586299-perceptions-germanys-chancel-
lor-who-likely-win-re-election-september-22nd-are.

Berlin Wall Memorial. "The Border Fortifications in the
Eighties." http://www.berliner-mauer-gedenkstaette.de/
en/aufbau-der-grenzanlagen-49.html.

Bernstein, Richard. "Merkel Takes Over as Germany's
Chancellor." *The International New York Times*,
November 22, 2005. http://www.nytimes.com/learning/
teachers/featured_articles/20051123wednesday.html.

Buergin, Rainer. "Merkel Says Balanced Budget, Energy
Take Priority in Third Term." *Bloomberg News*,
December 30, 2013. http://www.bloomberg.com/
news/2013-12-30/merkel-says-balanced-budget-
energy-take-priority-in-third-term.html.

Dempsey, Judy. "The Young Merkel: Idealist's Daughter." *The International New York Times*, September 6, 2005. http://www.nytimes.com/2005/09/05/world/europe/05iht-germany.html?scp=5&sq=kasner&st=cse&_r=0.

Deutschland.de. "Parties and Political Foundations." Accessed December 30, 2013. deutschland.de/en/topic/politics/germany-europe/parties-and-political-foundations.

Eddy, Melissa. "Merkel Offers a Peek Into Her Private Life." *The International New York Times*, May 17, 2013. http://www.nytimes.com/2013/05/18/world/europe/fascination-with-german-leaders-more-private-side.html.

European Commission. "Economic and Financial Affairs." Accessed December 29, 2013. http://ec.europa.eu/economy_finance/crisis/index_en.htm.

European Union. "The History of the European Union." Accessed December 22, 2013. http://europa.eu/about-eu/eu-history/index_en.htm.

European Union. "Towards a Single Currency: A Brief History of EMU." Accessed December 22, 2013. http://europa.eu/legislation_summaries/economic_and_monetary_affairs/introducing_euro_practical_aspects/l25007_en.htm.

Goldstein, Jacob. "The Crisis In Europe, Explained." *NPR*, June 4, 2012. http://www.npr.org/blogs/money/2012/06/04/154282337/the-crisis-in-europe-explained.

Howard, Caroline. "The World's Most Powerful Women 2013." *Forbes.com*, May 22, 2013.

Kornelius, Stefan. *Angela Merkel: The Chancellor and Her World*. Richmond, United Kingdom: Alma Books Ltd., 2013.

Mangasarian, Leon. "How Germany's Election System Works: What to Watch for Tomorrow" Bloomberg News, September 25, 2009. http://www.bloomberg.com/apps/news?pid=newsarchive&sid=aBSHoe_o5NX8.

Marr, Andrew. *The Making of Angela Merkel, a German Enigma*. London: BBC News, 2013. Television documentary.

Oltermann, Philip and Kate Connolly. "Angela Merkel Triumphs in German Election to Secure Historic Third Term." *The Guardian*, September 23, 2013. http://www.theguardian.com/world/2013/sep/23/german-election-angela-merkel.

Peel, Quentin. "Angela Merkel: A Woman of Power." *Financial Times*, December 14, 2012. http://www.ft.com/intl/cms/s/2/347c8b84-44b2-11e2-8fd7-00144feabdc0.html.

Raffaelli, Rosa. "The European Parliament: Historical Background." Fact sheets on the European Union, July, 2013. http://www.europarl.europa.eu/ftu/pdf/en/FTU_1.3.1.pdf.

Smale, Alison. "The Making of Angela Merkel." *The International New York Times*, October 30, 2012. http://rendezvous.blogs.nytimes.com/2012/10/30/the-making-of-angela-merkel/.

"Timeline: The Unfolding Eurozone Crisis." *BBC News*, June 13, 2012. http://www.bbc.co.uk/news/business-13856580.

Wiliarty, Sarah Elise. *The CDU and the Politics of Gender in Germany: Bringing Women to the Party*. Cambridge, England: Cambridge University Press, 2010.

INDEX

ABOUT THE AUTHOR

Tonya Maddox Cupp earned her English degree from Westminster College, the very institution where Winston Churchill gave his "Iron Curtain" speech. She was raised in Fulton, Missouri, and grew up immersed in history. She has been published by the Missouri Philological Association. She has also edited works for such educational publishers as John Wiley & Sons, Inc. and Pearson PLC. In addition to hanging out with her husband and daughter, she likes to read voraciously.